Path of Fury

The June 1, 2011 Tornado Left a 39-Mile Trail of
Devastation Through Western and Central Massachusetts

Presented by

The Republican.

Published by Pediment Publishing, a division of The Pediment Group, Inc. www.pediment.com Printed in Canada

Acknowledgments

THIS BOOK IS LARGELY THE work of the dedicated photographers and reporters at The Republican who were at the scene within minutes as the deadly June 1, 2011 tornado smashed into downtown Springfield just blocks from the Main Street office of the newspaper.

We had a lot of help in telling this story from our readers who submitted photos of the tornado to the pilots who got our photographers in the air to view the massive scope of the destruction along a 39-mile path. Special thanks to Mike Foy, whose law office was destroyed by the storm. Foy, also a pilot and co-owner of Westfield Flight Academy flew photographer John Suchocki back and forth to obtain many of the fantastic aerials in this book.

Special recognition should also go to the thousands of volunteers, rescue workers and emergency personnel who answered the call to help those impacted by the tornado. These photos help document their role.

This book is especially dedicated to those most affected by the tornado, many of whom lost everything, and to the families of those who were killed and injured.

Portions of the proceeds of this book will be shared by the Pioneer Valley Chapter of the American Red Cross which helped care for and shelter victims of the storm.

In the communities of Westfield, Agawam, West Springfield, Springfield, Wilbraham, Monson, Brimfield, Sturbridge, Southbridge and Charlton—the path of the tornado – hundreds of stories about neighbors helping neighbors and total strangers pitching in have surfaced. Out of a disaster came hope and a renewed faith in each other.

Wayne E. Phaneuf
Executive Editor
The Republican

Traveling the Path of Fury

THE FORECAST FOR JUNE 1, 2011 called for a humid day with a chance for some showers and thunderstorms. The humid air would be replaced by cooler temperatures and a nice stretch of weather. The forecast ended with:

"You'll be able to open up the windows and enjoy!"

By the end of that afternoon, hundreds of people didn't have windows, many didn't even have homes.

At 4:17 p.m. a tornado touched down in the southeast corner of Westfield and for the next hour and 10 minutes it would carve a long path of destruction, passing through Agawam, West Springfield, Springfield, Wilbraham, Monson, Brimfield, Sturbridge and finally ending at the Southbridge-Charlton line in Worcester County. In its wake it would leave nearly 350 homes and businesses destroyed and more than 1,500 damaged. Three

people lost their lives and less than 100 were injured. Damage was in the hundreds of millions of dollars.

Although the storm system spawned three tornadoes, two of them were minor and took down only trees in non-populated areas.

The principal tornado would have been a monster wherever it landed. It had a path 39 miles long. It was categorized as a F3, with winds of 158-206 mph

According to the National Weather Service Storm Prediction Center, from 1981 to 2010 in the United States, the median path length of tornadoes – half were longer, half were shorter – was just a half mile.

More than 1,200 tornadoes touch down in the United States each year, more than in any other country. Perhaps two or three materialize in Massachusetts each year and are usually a weak short-lived phenomena.

Along the path of the June 1 tornado were stories

of heroism, fear, faith and resolve.

The clock found on the gym floor of storm-damaged Munger Hill School in Westfield is stopped at 4:16 p.m., less than a minute from the official arrival of the tornado on the ground. Although many trees were leveled and 250 homes received some damage, Westfield escaped the full wrath of the storm. Only three homes received extensive damage and one was condemned. Within seconds the tornado exited the small slice of Westfield and headed into wooded areas of Agawam where it leveled hundreds of trees in Robinson State Park.

Although the tornado only hit a corner of West Springfield north of Memorial Avenue it devastated a neighborhood. The first call to the fire department was logged at 4:31 p.m. Two of the three fatalities from the huge storm occurred within a few blocks. Sergey Livchin, 23, died when a tree crushed his car

on Main Street. Angelica Guerrero, 39, died when her triple-decker house collapsed. She was shielding her 15-year-old daughter, Ibone, as they huddled in the bathtub. The city condemned 14 of the 186 buildings that had been damaged.

The tornado crossed the Connecticut River, slicing over the Memorial Bridge which was packed with rush-hour traffic. It just missed City Hall, tore through Court Square and slammed into the city's South End, one of the most densely populated neighborhoods in Springfield. Houses, apartment blocks, businesses and the historic Howard Street Armory, home of the South End Community Center were badly damaged or destroyed.

The path continued through the heart of the city, up Central Street to the Springfield College campus and over Watershops Pond into the East Forest Park neighborhood where it leveled several homes. By the time it exited Springfield from Tinkham Road in Sixteen Acres, it had damaged 1,000 buildings. Nearly 200 were demolished or condemned.

In Wilbraham the storm followed Tinkham Road, just missing the $67 million new high school under construction and crossing over Main Street and up the mountain into Monson. In Wilbraham, 234 homes were damaged, 13 were declared unsafe for habitation.

The tornado seemed to pick up strength as it barreled over the mountains right into the heart of Main Street in Monson. It smashed the Bethany Road neighborhood where one home was turned upside town and others obliterated. The town reported 51 properties were total losses and another 67 were badly damaged. Houses on every road the tornado crossed received severe damage.

It traveled through the Brimfield State Forest where it leveled half of the 3,000-acre woodland.

The third death of the storm occurred in Brimfield at Village Green Campground where Virginia Darlow, 52, was killed in her camper. The town building inspector reported 39 buildings were condemned. Some had been flattened.

The storm headed over East Brimfield Reservoir and into Sturbridge where it just missed the buildings of Old Sturbridge Village, crossed Route 131 and damaged the Fisk Hill area. Five structures, including a motel were condemned.

Before loosing its power in Southbridge, the tornado significantly damaged 76 buildings and wrecked several planes at the Southbridge Airport. Its 39-mile path of destruction finally over.

Many consider it a miracle that more people were not killed or injured.

— Wayne E. Phaneuf

Path of Destruction

THE MAP BELOW SHOWS THE 39-MILE SWATH OF DESTRUCTION THE TORNADO MADE FROM WESTFIELD TO THE SOUTHBRIDGE-CHARLTON LINE DURING ITS ONE HOUR AND 10 MINUTES ON THE GROUND.

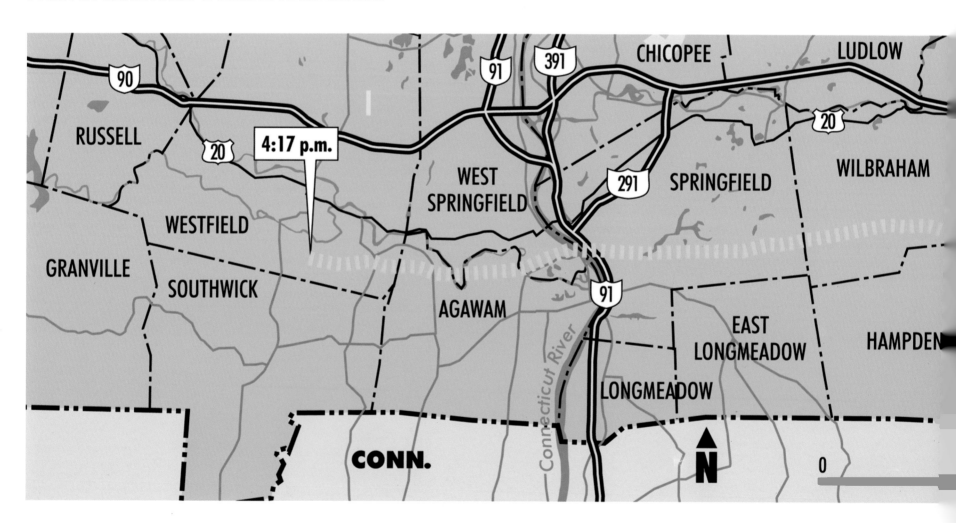

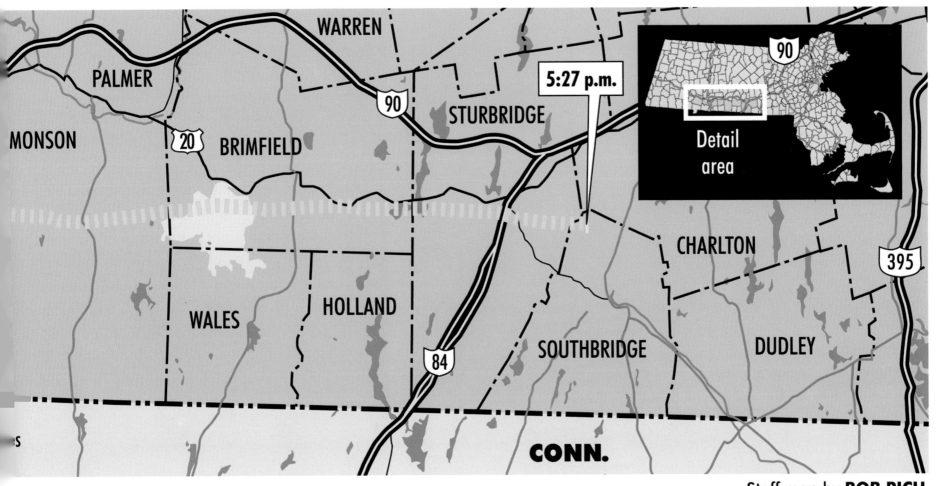

WARREN

PALMER

MONSON

90

STURBRIDGE

20 BRIMFIELD

5:27 p.m.

90

Detail area

CHARLTON

395

WALES HOLLAND

84

SOUTHBRIDGE

DUDLEY

s

CONN.

Staff map by **BOB RICH**

ABOVE: The tornado moving through Springfield as seen from North Main Street, East Longmeadow looking towards Granby Street as the tornado passes thru East Forest Park in the background.

Photo by Streetve Fournier

OPPOSITE LEFT: Tornado in downtown Springfield. *Photo by John J Garvey*

OPPOSITE RIGHT: Tornado slipping behind Monarch building. *Photo by John J Garvey*

ABOVE: Seniors hustle into the MassMutal Center in Springfield for the Minnechaug Regional High School prom Wednesday, June 1, 2011, despite the tornadoes that had traversed the area. *Photo by Dave Roback*

ABOVE: Debris surrounds St. Michaels Academy and Cathedral High on Wendover Road as more storm clouds move in. *Photo by Mark Murray*

LEFT: Bishop with children from St. Michaels Academy.

Photo by Mark Murray

BELOW: Memorial Bridge in West Springfield following the tornado.

Photo by Pamela Arwady

ABOVE: A piece of wood is stuck into the side of a car that was parked out front of Cathedral High on Surrey Road. *Photo by Mark Murray*

ABOVE: A boy with a dog looks at a building that collapsed on Central Street in the aftermath of the first tornado that ripped through Springfield. *Photo by Michael S. Gordon*

The Republican.

THURSDAY
JUNE 2, 2011

©2011 The Republican Co.

WWW.MASSLIVE.COM

75 cents

High 72 Low 49
Weather
Mostly sunnier and cooler./A16

NEWS TO GO
A QUICK RUN THROUGH SOME OF TODAY'S TOP STORIES

Vigil planned
A candlelight vigil is being planned for Friday on the town common to remember Tyler McNeill, the 15-year-old Belchertown High School freshman whose mother said took his own life. His mother has appealed to friends through Facebook about what might have been bothering the teen./**A9**

Mother charged
A pregnant Springfield mother was accused of dealing crack cocaine and other drug charges after police raided her home Tuesday night. Springfield detectives conducted a month-slong investigation into activities at the woman's home prior to the raid and arrest./**A12**

Murder trial opens
Opening arguments were made Wednesday in the fatal shooting trial of Shadeed J. Mahdi, who is accused of shooting Tory Lamont Smith in September 2009. The Girard Avenue incident led to the lock-down of Rebecca Johnson School./**A12**

Space transformed
The former Onyx Fusion Restaurant on Springfield's West Columbus Avenue is in the midst of being transformed into Mama Iguana's, a Mexican restaurant owned by Northampton restauranteur Claudio Guerra. Artists are finishing Mexican art to adorn the space./ **C1**

DEVASTATION

Two die as tornadoes hit area

By JACK FLYNN
jflynn@repub.com

SPRINGFIELD – Two tornadoes ripped through Greater Springfield Wednesday, killing two while carving a trail of destruction from West field to Sturbridge.

In the worst tornado outbreak in a century, nine communities were battered by back-to-back storms that left extensive damage and 38,000 homes without power late Wednesday night. As emergency workers searched neighborhoods for people trapped in homes or cars, Gov. Deval L. Patrick declared a state of emergency, called up 1,000 National Guard troops to help with the recovery, and planned to visit Springfield late Wednesday night.

One death was reported in West Springfield where a woman was killed when a tree crushed a car on Main Street, and one in Brimfield, according to the Massachusetts Emergency Management Agency.

The first funnel cloud touched down in Springfield at 4:30 p.m., battering downtown and the South End before slicing across East Forest Park and Sixteen Acres.'

Brenda J. Gooch said she and coworkers saw the tornado forming over West Springfield from her perch on the 13th floor of First Financial Plaza overlooking Court Square where she works for Boston Medical.

Please see Region, Page A3

INSIDE
Powerful twister hits Wilbraham, Page A3

Personnel open command center, Page A3

Storms postpone WMass volleyball tournament, Page B1

Staff photo by MICHAEL S. GORDON
Police respond to the aftermath after a tornado cut through Main Street in the South End of Springfield on Wednesday afternoon. Photo gallery and videos at MassLive.com.

Witnesses describe power of twisters

By JIM KINNEY
jkinney@repub.com

SPRINGFIELD – Sandra E. Blaney saw the trees on Bliss Street bending in the wind and thinking to herself: "Those trees are pretty old. There is no way they could break."

Blaney had just moved to Northampton from New York City. She's had her new job at Johnson and Hill Staffing for less than a month. She's only had her 2011 Subaru a few weeks.

And now she was stuck in traffic with a funnel cloud bearing down her.

"I closed my eyes," she said "I didn't want to see what was going to happen."

But she felt the car windows break inward. She felt the shards of broken glass hit her arms and neck. When she opened her eyes, the parking lot seemed a wasteland, she said. Cars were destroyed. Trees down. Bricks from nearby buildings littered the ground.

Blaney said she saw injured people. She was unhurt.

"I'm just shaken up. Shaking like a leaf," she said. She'd just started a job in Manhattan on Sept. 11, 2001.

"This reminded me of that terrible day," she said.

Further south, the area around Howard Street was transformed into a war zone, with bricks from the heavily-damaged South End Community Center littering the

Please see Views, Page A3

Staff photo by DON TREEGER
A child runs for cover on Central Street as bad weather moves back into area following a tornado touch-down in the South End of Springfield on Wednesday.

Tornadoes fail to stop prom

By STEPHANIE BARRY
sbarry@repub.com

SPRINGFIELD – Chan Thar Pye Sone, a senior at Minnechaug Regional High School, scratched at least one item off his bucket list on Wednesday: Surviving a tornado in a tuxedo.

He was among more than a 100 students who made it to the prom at the MassMutual Center in downtown Springfield just about two hours after one of several tornadoes ripped through parts of the city and the region.

Prom-goers shared the venue with about 500 bereft and bedraggled evacuees from city neighborhoods who lost their homes to the twister.

Storm victims were confined to the first floor while a continuous parade of limousines pulled up and deposited giddy teens in front of the Main Street

Please see Prom, Page A3

Staff photo by DAVE ROBACK
Seniors hustle into the MassMutal Center in Springfield for the Minnechaug Regional High School prom Wednesday despite the tornadoes that had traversed the area.

ABOVE: Cars are overturned on the front lawn of St. Michael's Academy on Wendover Road. *Photo by Mark Murray*

OPPOSITE: A child runs for cover on Central Street as bad weather moves back into the area following a tornado touch-down in the South End of Springfield on Wednesday. *Photo by Don Treeger*

BELOW: Damaged cars from wind and falling debris in the aftermath of the first tornado that ripped through Springfield. *Photo by Michael S. Gordon*

ABOVE: Apartments exposed by blown out walls of an apartment building on Hubbard Avenue in the aftermath of the first tornado that ripped through Springfield. *Photo by Michael S. Gordon*

OPPOSITE: The tornado path scene from Wendover Road in Springfield showing Roosevelt Avenue on Wednesday afternoon. *Photo by Mark Murray*

ABOVE: Tornado damage along Main Street in the South End. *Photo by Don Treeger*

LEFT: Damaged street sign in the South End. *Photo by Don Treeger*

ABOVE: Springfield police strategize on Main Street after a tornado hit the South End. *Photo by Don Treeger*

LEFT: A bystander reacts to tornado damage while scurrying for cover as another tornado approached. *Photo by Don Treeger*

FAR LEFT: View of tornado damage along Main Street in the South End. *Photo by Don Treeger*

ABOVE: Salvatore Rinaldi of Agawam just missed getting hit by a large oak tree as he drove up Maple Street during the first tornado that ripped through Springfield Wednesday afternoon. *Photo by Michael S. Gordon*

ABOVE: Overturned cars in front of St. Michaels Academy on Wendover Road. *Photo by Mark Murray*

ABOVE LEFT: Springfield police officers yell into buildings to see if anyone needs help on Main Street in the South End. *Photo by Don Treeger*

LEFT: Tornado damage along Central Street.

Photo by Don Treeger

ABOVE: The inside of the South End Community Center which lost most of its roof in the first tornado that ripped through Springfield. *Photo by Michael S. Gordon*

LEFT: The interior of the South End Community Center in the aftermath of the first tornado that ripped through Springfield. *Photo by Michael S. Gordon*

FAR LEFT: A smashed car sits next to the South End Community Center which lost most of its roof in the aftermath of the first tornado that ripped through Springfield. *Photo by Michael S. Gordon*

LEFT: A car traveling down Main Street in West Springfield is crushed by a fallen tree during Wednesday's storm. The driver was killed.

Photo by Dave Roback

OPPOSITE: The Ames House at MacDuffie School damaged during the first tornado that ripped through Springfield Wednesday afternoon. *Photo by Michael S. Gordon*

BELOW LEFT: Trees are down in and buildings are damaged on Union Street in West Springfield.

Photo by Dave Roback

BELOW RIGHT: Munger Hill Elementary School had a section of the roof torn off during Wednesday's storms. Here is one of the kindergarten classes.

Photo by Manon L. Mirabelli

ABOVE: Storm damage at Ross and Theresa Rodgers' home at 61 Pontoosic Road in Westfield. *Photo by Manon L. Mirabelli*

LEFT: Storm damage at Ross and Theresa Rodgers' home at 61 Pontoosic Road in Westfield. *Photo by Manon L. Mirabelli*

BELOW LEFT: Car are overturned in front of St. Michael's Academy off Wendover Road in Springfield. *Photo by Mark Murray*

BELOW RIGHT: A former parking attendant booth off of Howard Street in Springfield.

Photo by Dave Roback

ABOVE: The roof at Cathedral High was damaged and windows blown out as a result of the storm. *Photo by Mark Murray*

LEFT: Roof from Cathedral High is on Wendover Road. *Photo by Mark Murray*

OPPOSITE: A few branches are all that remains to this tree on Wendover Road near Cathedral High School. *Photo by Mark Murray*

RIGHT: Main Street in the South End in the aftermath of the first tornado that ripped through Springfield Wednesday afternoon. *Photo by Michael S. Gordon*

OPPOSITE: Springfield Police go door to door checking for people trapped inside of houses and apartment buildings on Central Street in the aftermath of the first tornado that ripped through Springfield.

Photo by Michael S. Gordon

BELOW LEFT: The side of the South End Community Center in Springfield. *Photo by Dave Roback*

BELOW RIGHT: A couple stops to look at the storm damage in front of St. Michael's Academy on Wendover Road. *Photo by Mark Murray*

ABOVE: Trees are down in Springfield's historic Court Square. *Photo by Dave Roback*

ABOVE LEFT: Tree down and buildings damaged on the MacDuffie School campus on Maple Street in the aftermath of the first tornado that ripped through Springfield Wednesday afternoon. *Photo by Michael S. Gordon*

BELOW LEFT: Trees are down in Springfield's historic Court Square. *Photo by Dave Roback*

ABOVE: The exterior of the South End Community Center in the aftermath of the first tornado that ripped through Springfield Wednesday afternoon. *Photo by Michael S. Gordon*

RIGHT: Tornado damage along Central Street in the South End. *Photo by Don Treeger*

ABOVE: Reynalis Mathews is seen with her mom Cynthia Gonzalez at the shelter at the MassMutual Center in Springfield. *Photo by Dave Roback*

OPPOSITE: An 11:00 pm press conference at the Raymond Sullivan Safety complex of the Springfield Fire Department Wednesday following a series of tornadoes in the area, state, city and federal officials spoke about the disaster. From left, Massachusett Lt. Gov. Timothy P. Murray, U. S. Sen. John F. Kerry, D-Mass., Gov. Deval Patrick and Springfield Mayor Domenic J. Sarno. *Photo by Michael S. Gordon*

TORNADO EXTRA

The Republican.

THURSDAY,
JUNE 2, 2011

Big Y's Famous
BUY ONE GET TWO FREE
SALE STARTS JUNE 2, 2011

©2011 The Republican Co. ——— **WWW.MASSLIVE.COM** ——— 75 cents

STATE OF EMERGENCY

The tornado path scene from Wendover Road in Springfield showing Roosevelt Avenue on Wednesday afternoon. Storm photo galleries and videos at MassLive.com.

Staff photo by **MARK M. MURRAY**

Two die as tornadoes hit area

By JACK FLYNN and JEANETTE DeFORGE
Staff writers

SPRINGFIELD – Two tornadoes ripped through Greater Springfield Wednesday, killing two, injuring dozens and carving a corridor of destruction from Westfield to Sturbridge.

In the region's worst tornado outbreak in a century, 10 communities were battered by back-to-back storms that inflicted widespread damage and left 57,000 homes without power Wednesday night.

With emergency workers searching for people trapped in homes and cars, Gov. Deval L. Patrick declared a state of emergency, called up 1,000 National Guard troops, and traveled to Springfield late Wednesday night to view the storm damage.

One death was reported in Brimfield, where at least two other residents are missing, state police said. The second fatality came in West Springfield, where a falling tree crushed a woman's car on Main Street.

In Monson, the steeple of the First Church of Monson was sheared off as the funnel cloud swirled through town, stripping limbs from trees, chimneys from roofs and roofs from houses.

By early evening, the tornadoes had skipped through at least 10 communities – Agawam, Charlton, Monson, Oxford, Springfield, West Springfield, Westfield, Wilbraham, Brimfield and Sturbridge – and left more than 50,000 people without power.

National Grid said a helicopter would be used today to assess dam-

Please see Region, Page A13

INSIDE

Seeing is believing for storm witnesses, Page A9

Powerful twister hits Wilbraham, Page A10

Area hospitals set for disaster, Page A10

Damaging storm 'uncharacteristic,' Page A10

Personnel open command center, Page A10

Storms postpone WMass volleyball tournament, Page B1

The steeple of the First Church of Monson lays in rubble on the ground after a tornado swept through the downtown area of Monson on Wednesday.

Officials pledge aid to clean up Springfield

By ROBERT RIZZUTO
rizzuto@repub.com

SPRINGFIELD – Western Massachusetts will receive help from state and federal agencies as local crews work in the wake of the tornadoes that devastated much of the area Wednesday.

At a press conference held at the city's Emergency Pre-

paredness Center on Carew Street late Wednesday night, local officials were joined by Gov. Deval Patrick and Sen. John Kerry, who both assured Western Massachusetts that help in on the streets and more is on the way.

Springfield Mayor Domenic Sarno confirmed that more than 40 people have been hospitalized due to injuries sus-

tained in the tornadoes, and Patrick confirmed that there were four fatalities. The Republican confirmed two in West Springfield and Brimfield.

"This basically started out in West Springfield, moved over the bridge and really has done a devastating job on our South End. Then it went over to East Forest Park and Six-

teen Acres," Sarno said. "We were hit again in the Indian Orchard area and are still trying to confirm if we were hit another time."

Schools in Hampden, Springfield, Westfield, and Wilbraham are closed today and Sarno dismissed all nonessential city employees from their duties for the day.

Kerry expressed his condo-

lences to the families affected and said the victims will be served by a "unified response."

"When I first talked to the governor, he was in the bunker in Framingham and he was with officials from the Federal Emergency Management Administration. Emergency

Please see Help, Page A12

Index

Business	B8	Obituaries	A22
Classified	B6	Scoreboard	B5
Golf	B4	Sports	B1
Nation	A14	Weather	A24

RIGHT: The damaged apartment building at 323 Central Street.

Photo by Michael S. Gordon

FAR RIGHT: A damaged house on Central Street.

Photo by Michael S. Gordon

ABOVE: The tower of the Naismith Memorial Basketball Hall of Fame is visible behind an apartment building in the city's South End. *Photo by Michael S. Gordon*

OPPOSITE: A badly damaged house at 374 Hancock Street. *Photo by Michael S. Gordon*

ABOVE: The family and friends of Izetta J. Fleming clean debris from around her house on hard hit Beech Street.   *Photo by Michael S. Gordon*

ABOVE: Anita Rivera moves wood from in front of her house on Beech Street. *Photo by Michael S. Gordon*

ABOVE: Pedestrians walked by a house that was lifted off its foundation and badly damaged on Beech Street. *Photo by Michael S. Gordon*

RIGHT: Jesus Delgado rests in front of a house on Central Street.
Photo by Michael S. Gordon

BELOW: Vincent Travi of Hollow Road, Brimfield trying to salvage items from his home that was completely destroyed by the tornado. His wife Cindy was home when it hit and survived in the basement by holding onto part of the concrete foundation.

Photo by Don Treeger

ABOVE: A badly damaged house at 374 Hancock Street. *Photo by Michael S. Gordon*

LEFT: A badly damaged house on Pine Street Court. *Photo by Michael S. Gordon*

ABOVE: A man pushes bricks and wood from the top of a house on Central Street. *Photo by Michael S. Gordon*

OPPOSITE: Residents begin the clean up work on hard hit Beech Street. *Photo by Michael S. Gordon*

ABOVE: Badly damaged houses on Pine Street Court. *Photo by Michael S. Gordon*

ABOVE: The badly damaged home of Enelida Reyes on Pine Street Court.

Photo by Michael S. Gordon

ABOVE: Patrick A. Plunkett, left, co-owner of J P Auto Repair on Central Street in the city's South End, along with Garnett Dun Kelly, surveys the destruction of the garage, damaged when a tornado ripped through Springfield Wednesday afternoon. He and worker Richard Ricketts, at right, sought shelter in the office when the tornado hit.

Photo by Michael S. Gordon

LEFT: Springfield firefighters remove loose building material from apartment buildings on Central Street.

Photo by Michael S. Gordon

ABOVE: Tornado aftermath in Monson: The steeple of the First Church of Monson lies in ruins on the lawn of the church. *Photo by Don Treeger*

RIGHT: Bilenia Belen, holds her daughter Roselic Perez 9 month old, as her sons Mobesto David 11, and Jesus David 7, get settled in at the Shelter set up at the MassMutual Center for storm victims.

Photo by Mark Murray

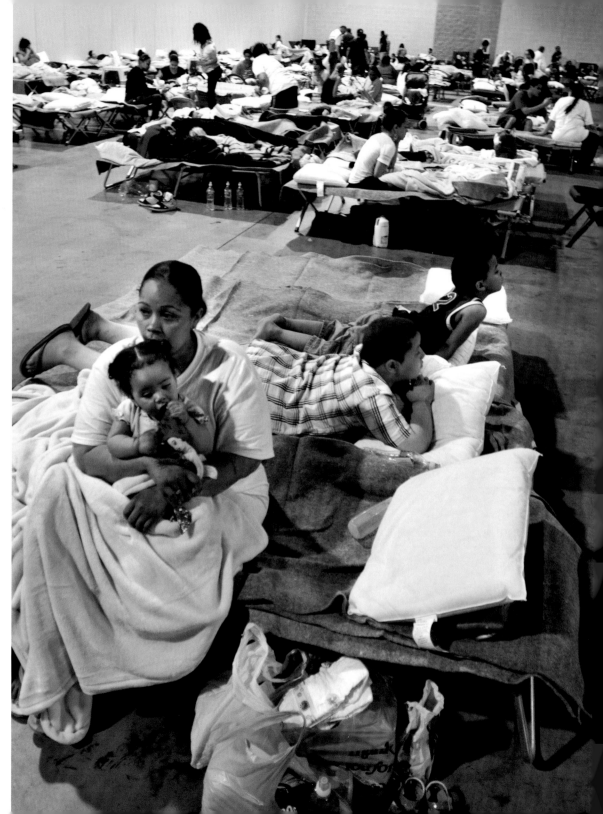

LEFT: Tornado aftermath in Brimfield: Barbara and David Minney of Ware search for items to salvage from the home of their son Brett Minney of Hollow Road, Brimfield. Brett was inside the mobile home when the tornado lifted it off the foundation and smashed it to the ground. *Photo by Don Treeger*

BELOW LEFT: Tornado aftermath in Brimfield: People try to salvage what is left from a horse barn and apartment on Hollow Road. *Photo by Don Treeger*

BELOW RIGHT: Tornado aftermath in Wilbraham: This is an inside view of the Bredvik home on Echo Hill Road. There used to be two sliding doors in the doorway. *Photo by Don Treeger*

ABOVE: Damage on Echo Hill Road in Wilbraham. *Photo by Don Treeger*

ABOVE: With the First Church of Monson's steeple laying in ruins on the ground a Sunday morning church service, the first since the June 1 tornado damage the church and the town, took place inside the old church. *Photo by David Molnar*

ABOVE: Pia M. Rogers sits on the foundation of her former house at 14 Bethany Road in Monson that was destroyed in Wednesday's tornado. Next to her are family friends, left to right, Jake Dold and Kyle Table, both 14 from Monson. *Photo by Lori Streetbile*

RIGHT: Tornado aftermath in Monson: This a view from Ely Road looking down on storm damage near downtown Monson.

Photo by Don Treeger

BELOW: A house turned upside down on Stewart Avenue in Monson by Wednesday's tornado. *Photo by Lori Streetbile*

ABOVE: Tornado aftermath in Wilbraham: This is a view of the Bredvik house on Echo Hill Road. *Photo by Don Treeger*

ABOVE RIGHT: Tornado aftermath in Wilbraham: Here, Dr. Brian Bredvik tosses bed linens down to a friend as he salvages items from his Echo Hill Rd. home. *Photo by Don Treeger*

RIGHT: Path of tornado looking west from East Brimfield Reservoir, June 2, 2011. *Photo by John Suchocki*

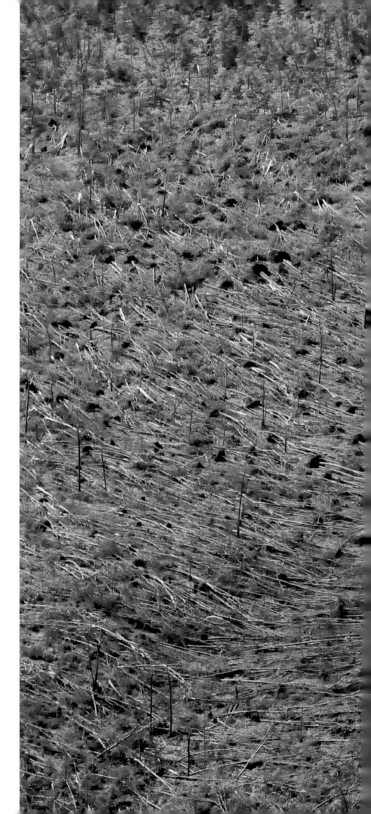

ABOVE: Springfield East Forest Park homes damaged by the tornado.

Photo by John Suchocki

RIGHT: Kim Slozak stands in front of her house at 6 Bethany Road in Monson. *Photo by Lori Stabile*

FAR RIGHT: Monson area forest damaged by the tornado.

Photo by John Suchocki

ABOVE: Laura Yarbrough stands in front of her destroyed home in Monson. *Photo by Lori Stabile*

OPPOSITE: Heather L. Emery hugs Russell Bressette Jr. Bressette lost his home on Stewart Avenue in Monson. *Photo by Lori Stabile*

BELOW: Damage at Adams Market in Monson. *Photo by Lori Stabile*

ABOVE: Monson home of Judi Bedell turned upside down by tornado. *Photo by John Suchocki*

LEFT: Springfield College dorms damaged by tornado. *Photo by John Suchocki*

ABOVE: Debris from various homes is scattered along Pennsylvania Avenue in the East Forest Park section of Springfield ,which was hit hard by the tornado. *Photo by Mark M. Murray*

OPPOSITE TOP LEFT: Anna Lin of Monson looks over her destroyed home at 15 Bethany Road.

Photo by Lori Streetbile

OPPOSITE BOTTOM LEFT: Patty Faerrarini of 413 Roosevelt Avenue poses with a statue of St. Joseph that she found in her yard while clearing some fallen trees. She has never seen the statue before and believes it was dropped on the storm after being carried by the wind from Cathedral High School several hundred yards away. *Photo by Patrick Johnson*

OPPOSITE RIGHT: Unitarian Universalist parish of Monson on Main Street where the steeple has been ripped off. *Photo by Lori Streetbile*

ABOVE: Rubble from the building at 667-669 Union Street which took the life of a woman, is slammed up against the building next door, including a car which was pushed into the wall. *Photo by Mark M. Murray*

ABOVE: A woman talks with National Guard soldiers patrolling Roosevelt Avenue in Springfield. *Photo by Mark M. Murray*

LEFT: Michael Bynum sits on the chimney of his house at 110 Pennsylvania Avenue in the East Forest Park section of Springfield, which was blown away with him inside it during yesterday's tornado. He received injuries as a result of the hit. All that is left of his home is the cellar hole. *Photo by Mark M. Murray*

BELOW: Former Westfield Mayor Michael Boulanger removes one of the trees that snapped in his yard on Glernwood Drive. The back is his neighbor's house took the brunt of the damage.

Photo by Michael Beswick

ABOVE: Barbara Fields, New England Regional Manager for the United States Department of Housing and Urban Development, center, tours Main Street in the South End with Congressman Richard E. Neal, D-Mass., left, and Springfield Mayor Domenic J. Sarno, right. *Photo by Michael S. Gordon*

RIGHT: Rubble sits on the front lawn of this house on East Forest Park section of Springfield. *Photo by Mark M. Murray*

OPPOSITE: Homes on Stewart Avenue, Monson, with heavy equipment starting the demolition on the homes destroyed by the tornado. *Photo by John Suchocki*

BELOW: The Salvation Army Disaster van drives up Wendover Road past the damage at Cathedral High School. *Photo by Mark M. Murray*

ABOVE: Tornado aftermath in Monson: Sen. John F. Kerry and Gov. Deval L. Patrick look over damage to the First Church of Monson. *Photo by Don Treeger*

LEFT: Springfield Main Street businesses damaged by the tornado. *Photo by John Suchocki*

ABOVE: Storm damage on Russell Street in West Springfield. *Photo by Don Treeger*

BELOW: Cars stacked in a lot off Union Street, West Springfield, from the tornado on Wednesday. *Photo by John Suchocki*

The Republican.

FRIDAY
JUNE 3, 2011

©2011 The Republican Co. · · · **WWW.MASSLIVE.COM** · · · 75 cents

AFTERMATH

Tornado death toll 3; federal aid sought

High 70 Low 42
Weather
Today will be breezy and cool with a good deal of sunshine./A20

NEWS TO GO
A QUICK RUN THROUGH SOME OF TODAY'S TOP STORIES

Monson hard hit
The tornadoes cut a path through Monson, leveling trees on Ely Road, sweeping through the downtown and knocking off the roofs of the town office building and Adams IGA supermarket on Main Street. Damage was spread through the neighborhood behind the town offices, on State Street, Washington Street, Bethany Road and Stewart Avenue. Homes were heavily damaged, and, in some cases, missing altogether./A10

Woman's loss
Anita Rivera, a local Puerto Rican radio personality and founder of El Pueblo Latino, The Republican's weekly Spanish publication, was horrified when she pulled onto her street Wednesday afternoon and realized her home was falling apart. Her story will be told to readers of The Republican and, in Spanish, to readers of El Pueblo Latino./A14

Helping others
Many of those untouched by the tornado are hurt by the suffering they are seeing and are looking for ways to help. Charities have the answers./A12

Medical response
Health officials are giving good marks to hospital workers for their response to the tornadoes that swept through Western Massachusetts Wednesday leaving scores injured./A14

Staff photo by JOHN SUCHOCKI
A Monson home was ripped from its foundation at right and flipped upside down by a tornado Wednesday afternoon. This house on the left appears less damaged. To see photo galleries and videos, go to www.masslive.com.

Mother killed shielding teen

West Springfield's Merrick section was left a shambles by the tornado.

By SANDRA E. CONSTANTINE and GEORGE GRAHAM
sconstantine@repub.com

WEST SPRINGFIELD – A mother died shielding her 15-year-old daughter in a bathtub as their three-story apartment building on Union Street collapsed into rubble during Wednesday's tornado.

"There is no doubt she saved her daughter," Police Chief Thomas E. Burke said during a Thursday press conference in the Merrick section which was an eerie scene of destruction populated by police, utility workers, media and the curious.

Burke identified the 40-year-old mother as either Angelique or Angelica Guerrero. The tornado that ripped through and devastated the Merrick neighborhood also claimed the life of a 23-year-old man sitting in the driver's seat of his 2005 Kia parked along Main Street at Hill Street.

He said Sergey Livchin, of 15 LaBelle St., was pronounced dead at the scene, but a passenger in his Kia survived after a tree fell on the vehicle. The call came in to police about 4:45 p.m.

Guerrero's husband and daughter were taken to Baystate Medical Center in Springfield for treatment, he said. The daughter suffered cuts to her legs, the police chief said.

The mother and daughter were in the first-floor apartment of their three-family building in the vicinity of 687 Union St.

"The third floor is now in the cellar," Burke said.

The police chief said the husband was able to free himself from the wreckage and call out to neighbors for help. Firefighters freed the mother and daughter.

Only the brick and concrete front steps remain. Thursday, hard-hatted workers searched the remains for family valu-

Please see Mother, Page A4

Staff photo by MARK M. MURRAY
Michael Bynum sits on the chimney of his house at 110 Pennsylvania Ave. in the East Forest Park section of Springfield on Thursday. The house was blown away with Bynum inside during Wednesday's tornado. All that is left of the house is the cellar hole.

By JACK FLYNN and GEORGE GRAHAM
Staff writers

SPRINGFIELD – The number of dead rose to three from Wednesday's tornadoes as a dozen-storm ravaged communities launched recovery efforts and Massachusetts congressional delegation appealed to the White House for disaster relief.

In a letter to President Obama, U.S. Sen. John Kerry, U.S. Rep. Richard E. Neal and six delegation members called for a presidential disaster declaration needed to steer millions in federal aid to homeowners and businesses in central and Western Massachusetts.

The appeal came 18 hours after Gov. Deval Patrick declared a state of emergency after two late-afternoon tornadoes rained destruction on a dozen communities from Westfield to Sturbridge.

A third death - involving a West Springfield mother killed while shielding her 15-year old daughter in a bathtub - was confirmed Thursday, in addition to a West Springfield motorist crushed by a tree and woman camping in Brimfield.

Area hospitals treated about 80 patients suffering from minor injuries to lightning strikes and trauma; at Baystate Medical Center, two required surgery and a third, an assistant district attorney, remains in serious condition after being struck by debris.

No estimates have been provided for the total cost of the storms, but Kerry said he ex-

Please see Wake, Page A5

Insurance claims may take months

By JIM KINNEY
Business writer

SPRINGFIELD – Insurance adjusters converged on Western Massachusetts Thursday, but the hard work of sorting out insurance claims could take months.

Insurers also said Thursday that they have already started cutting checks to customers who need to replace clothing or move to a hotel room.

"The goal is to get the process started as quickly as possible," said Glenn A. Greenberg, spokesman for Liberty Mutual's home office in Boston. "We do have people in the field inspecting homes. But we know that those calls have only now just begun to come in. Some of these people don't have phone service or even cell-phone service."

Hartford-based The Travelers had 75 claims adjusters in

Woman recounts dire experience

By STEPHANIE BARRY
sbarry@repub.com

BRIMFIELD – Cindy Travi looked at the mountain of rubble that used to be her post-and-beam home at 28 Hollow Road and thought: What if?

What if she had not hit the

with her husband, Vincent, surveyed what was once their home early Thursday afternoon.

Travi said she had just planted a tomato bush outside when her mother-in-law called Wednesday warning her of an approaching torna-

ABOVE: House at the corner of Union and George Street where one of the two deaths in West Springfield occurred when the tornado hit. The flowers planted in the front of the house were untouched. *Photo by John Suchocki*

RIGHT: Springfield South End Community Center damaged by the tornado. *Photo by John Suchocki*

OPPOSITE: Kelly and Jim Graham work to salvage as much from the kitchen of what is left of their home at 29 Judith Street off Island Pond Road, Their home was destroyed and had to be taken down. *Photo by Mark M. Murray*

BELOW LEFT: Clean-up continues on Bridge Street in West Springfield.
Photo by Don Treeger

BELOW MIDDLE: House at 79 and 81 George Street was marked after a search was made. *Photo by John Suchocki*

BELOW RIGHT: Springfield Main Street businesses damaged by the tornado. *Photo by John Suchocki*

ABOVE: A trash barrel along with electric and telephone lines are tangled up in this tree on Rosella Street as a result of the tornado.

Photo by Mark M. Murray

ABOVE RIGHT: A home on Wales Road (Route 19) in Brimfield that was in the pathway of Wednesday's tornado. *Photo by Lori Streetbile*

RIGHT: Mail carrier Tom Brown tries unsuccessfully to deliver mail on Stewart Avenue in Monson Thursday. The street was decimated by the tornado, with home after home leveled. *Photo by Lori Stabilc*

LEFT: Walking down Washington Street with free water and work gloves are volunteers Davis Johnson, Donna Beck and Luke Sullivan all Monson residents and members of the First Church of Monson which was also damaged by the June 1 tornado. They were passing out the items to emergency crews and homeowners working to clean up three days after the tornado devastated the town. *Photo by David Molnar*

BELOW LEFT: Utility crews and construction crews work on the damaged homes and utility lines in Monson three days after the June 1 tornado.

Photo by David Molnar

BELOW RIGHT: From left to right, One Stop Towing and Classic Heaven owner David A. Bell gets a hug from friend Scott Cable of Holland. Bell's business on Holland Road in Brimfield was destroyed. All 70 vehicles were ruined by the tornado – classic cars, tow trucks, used cars, he said. The video his employee took of the tornado's aftermath at the went viral.

Photo by Lori Streetbile

ABOVE: Home owners, residents, relatives and friends help remove debris from a flattened home on Washington Street as the neighborhood clean ups on day three after the June 1 tornado. *Photo by David Molnar*

ABOVE: Someone placed small American flags in a tree trunk snapped by the June 1 tornado in Monson. *Photo by David Molnar*

LEFT: Tornado aftermath in downtown Springfield: This is Devon Boreland watching the house he owns get demolished on William Street due to tornado damage. *Photo by Don Treeger*

RIGHT: One of the scores of homes damaged or destroyed on Bethany Road in Monson after the June 1 tornado.

Photo by David Molnar

FAR RIGHT: Friends of the homeowner who lives on Bethany Road Linda Meacham, of New York, Jody and Richard Pierce, of Barre, MA help clean the cellar hole of a home that totally blew away on the third day of clean up after the June 1 tornado that devastated the town of Monson. *Photo by David Molnar*

ABOVE: Main Street building panorama showing the demolition of buildings damaged in the South End of Springfield. *Photo by John Suchocki*

RIGHT: Tinkham Road in Wilbraham with houses on Echo Hill Road seen the background on Monday after the tornado. *Photo by Dave Roback*

LEFT: Peter Payson III, Mike Kowal and Corey Mackie remove debris from Payson's home on Evangeline Drive in Wilbraham. Payson's son, Ian, age 11 rode out the storm in the families basement. *Photo by Dave Roback*

FAR LEFT: Vladimir Livchin stands at the roadside memorial at Main and Hill Streets to his son Sergey who was killed in the tornado. *Photo by Don Treeger*

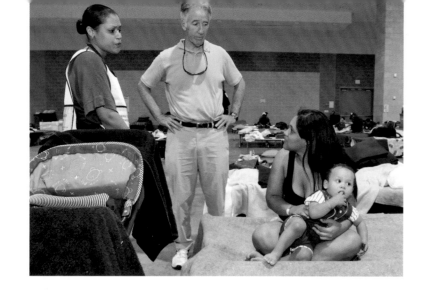

EDWARDS INDICTED ON CAMPAIGN FINANCE CHARGE/A3

The Republican.

SATURDAY
JUNE 4, 2011

©2011 The Republican Co.

WWW.MASSLIVE.COM

75 cents

RECOVERY BEGINS

High 76 Low 50
Weather
Sunshine with a few clouds./A14

NEWS TO GO
A QUICK RUN THROUGH SOME OF TODAY'S TOP STORIES

Bleak jobs report
A bleak jobs report suggests the recovery from the Great Recession will be longer and bumpier than many economists had envisioned. Most economists say job growth should strengthen later this year as gasoline prices drop further and the economy recovers from the effects of natural disasters in the U.S. and abroad. But the recovery is starting to weaken 17 months before the 2012 election./**A4**

'Gunsmoke' actor dies
James Arness, who portrayed Marshal Matt Dillon in the CBS-TV series "Gunsmoke," died Friday of natural causes. He was 88./**A7**

Federer advances
Roger Federer has ended Novak Djokovic's perfect season and 43-match winning streak, beating him 7-6 (5), 6-3, 3-6, 7-6 (5) in the French Open semifinals. Federer advanced to Sunday's title match against five-time champion Rafael Nadal. Nadal defeated Andy Murray 6-4, 7-5, 6-4 in Friday's other semifinal./**B1**

The good life
Inside The Republican today, Pioneer Valley Life Section D

FREE DOOR, CAR OR PET MAT
Boston Carpet
Redeem certificate in today's

Staff photo by MARK M. MURRAY
Kelly and Jim Graham work to salvage as much as possible from the kitchen of their tornado-ravaged home at 29 Louise St., off Island Pond Road in Springfield.

Officials promise disaster aid

By PATRICK JOHNSON and PETER GOONAN
Staff writers

SPRINGFIELD – The tornado that ripped through Springfield and other parts of Hampden County was the second strongest ever recorded in Massachusetts, with wind speeds estimated at 136 to 165 mph, an official with the National Weather Service said Friday.

Meteorologist Eleanor Vallier-Talbot with the National Weather Service said preliminary investigations show that in areas hardest hit, the tornado was estimated as an EF-3 on the Enhanced Fujita Damage Classification Scale.

The scale classifies tornadoes on a scale of 1-5 with 5 being the most intense. The tornado that flattened Joplin, Mo. last month was considered an EF-5 with winds in excess of 200 mph.

The highest rating recorded for a Massachusetts hurricane was one that struck Worcester in July, 1953, which had was an EF-4, she said.

And she cautioned the numbers for the Springfield tornado are preliminary.

"It could possibly go higher," she said.

The National Weather Service has determined there were actually three separate tornadoes. The most severe one was the EF-3 that carved a half-mile path for 39 miles from Westfield to Charlton. It killed

Please see **Tornado**, *Page A13*

INSIDE
Tornado aftermath photos, **Page A10**

Springfield Armor, Falcons join tornado relief effort. **Page B1**

Area starts long claims process

An insurance adjuster can handle only one or two claims a day taking the most serious cases first.

By JIM KINNEY
Business writer

SPRINGFIELD – Insurance adjuster David W. Valentine disappeared up through the closet and into the attic crawl space of 29 Rosella St. in the hard-hit East Forest Park neighborhood.

"I can hear his tape measure. That means he's still alive," joked homeowner Sean T. Wylie.

A few minutes later Valentine descended, flashlight in

hand. The prognosis was not good.

"You have at least one cracked rafter that I can see," Valentine, a property field trainer for The Travelers Cos. said. "Again, with more light I might be able to see more."

He'll only visit two or three homes Friday. He said it takes hours to navigate storm-clogged roads, and he likes to spend a lot of time with each homeowner. Another Travelers adjuster worked across the street while Valentine met with Wylie.

That splintered rafter meant that Valentine's original guess that Wylie's home had only suffered $5,000 to $10,000 in damage probably was too low.

Please see **Adjust**, *Page A13*

Staff photo by JIM KINNEY
David W. Valentine, right, a property field trainer for The Travelers Cos., points out damage at 29 Rosella St. in Springfield to homeowner Sean T. Wylie on Friday.

Downtown sites host graduates

By BRIAN STEELE
bsteele@repub.com

SPRINGFIELD – After observing a moment of silence for those affected by Wednesday's tornadoes, 291 Minnechaug Regional High School students graduated at Symphony Hall Friday.

Class president Andrew Johnston said the tornado should bring people closer.

"We have all

INSIDE
More graduations, **Page A8**

Staff photo by MICHAEL S. GORDON
Karmen A. DeCaro, left, and Anthony M. Bavaro pause for a self portrait before the start of the Minnechaug Regional High School graduation Friday night at Springfield Symphony Hall.

Assisted suicide advocate Kevorkian dies

By COREY WILLIAMS and ED WHITE
Associated Press

DETROIT – Jack Kevorkian built his suicide machine with parts gathered from flea markets and stashed it in a rusty Volkswagen van.

But it was Kevorkian's audacious attitude that set him apart in the debate over doctor-assisted suicide. The retired pathologist who said he

Jack Kevorkian

ABOVE: Volunteer James Demers of Brimfield, center, grills hamburgers for utility crews, residents and other volunteers helping clean up the town of Monson at the First Church of Monson which had it's steeple blown off by the June 1 tornado. *Photo by David Molnar*

OPPOSITE TOP LEFT: Congressman Richard E. Neal talks with Yuliana Ortiz and her one year old son Yulian at the shelter at the MassMutual Center. They lived on Adams Street and were displaced by the tornado. At left is interpreter Dionisia Lopez. *Photo by Don Treeger*

OPPOSITE TOP RIGHT: Electrical crews and Verizon crews line State Street in Monson repairing utility lines as crews clean up on day three after the June 1 tornado. *Photo by David Molnar*

OPPOSITE BOTTOM: Cots fill the exhibition hall at the MassMutual Center that is being used as a Red Cross shelter for tornado victims.

Photo by Don Treeger

ABOVE: The scene at 68 Haynes Hill Road in Brimfield.
Photo by Dave Roback

LEFT: With the damaged roof area tarped to protect the interior of the First Church of Monson a Sunday morning church service, the first since the June 1 tornado damage the church and the town, took place inside the old church. The tornado destroyed the church's steeple. *Photo by David Molnar*

BELOW: A sign of thanks sits at 76 Waid Road in Monson thanking folks for their help during the tornado and the aftermath. *Photo by Dave Roback*

ABOVE: The scene at 65 Haynes Hill Road in Brimfield. An American flag sits at the end of the driveway. *Photo by Dave Roback*

ABOVE: The post holding a basketball hoop behind Massasoit Hall on the Springfield College campus was bent over by the June 1 tornado that ripped through the area. In the background are houses damaged on Arcadia Boulevard. *Photo by Michael S. Gordon*

RIGHT: The fallen brick facade of the former Waterfront Lounge on Hickory Street damaged by the June 1 tornado that ripped through the area. *Photo by Michael S. Gordon*

ABOVE: Wood chips from the town of Wilbrahm are being piled up off of Post Office Park Road in Wilbraham on Monday. *Photo by Dave Roback*

LEFT: Playground equipment stands behind a housing project on Hickory Street damaged by the June 1 tornado that ripped through the area.

Photo by Michael S. Gordon

LEFT: A sense of humor is important to have as the owner of the home at 860 Plumtree Road, put a doll house complete with holes in the roof with stick and some spray paint on the side, as the real house in the background did receive heavy damage, but they found time for a light moment. *Photo by Mark M. Murray*

FAR LEFT: Justin J. Hurst of Springfield cuts up trees outside his cousin Bruce King's house on Melrose Street. *Photo by Michael S. Gordon*

ABOVE: Madeline R. Zorzi, owner of South Commons Condominium Association at 959-991 Main Street in the South End, walks by her properties now being demolished after they were damaged beyond repair during the June 1 tornado.

Photo by Michael S. Gordon

ABOVE RIGHT: The buildings at the corner of Main and Union and are now just rubble as crews started to knock them down after they received heavy tornado damage. *Photo by Mark M. Murray*

RIGHT: A pedestrian walks by wreckage of the June 1 tornado on Merrick Street, West Springfield, Wednesday. *Photo by Michael S. Gordon*

OPPOSITE: Homes on Haynes Hill Road in Brimfield ravaged by the June 1 tornadoes.

Photo by Lori Stabile

ABOVE: Homes off Echo Hill and Wildwood Lane and Tinkham Road in Wilbraham with tornado damage. *Photo by John Suchocki*

ABOVE RIGHT: Brookside Circle in Wilbraham with tornado damage. *Photo by John Suchocki*

RIGHT: Westfield at Munger Hill Elementary School where the tornado first touched down.
Photo by John Suchocki

FAR RIGHT: Clark Street, Spruce Street, Central Street and Hancock Street area of damage in Springfield. *Photo by John Suchocki*

ABOVE: Old First Church in the center of Monson in the center right with the trees blown down leading into the town from the top of the photo. *Photo by John Suchocki*

LEFT: Downtown Monson at State Street and Washington Street showing the damage from the tornados winds. *Photo by John Suchocki*

ABOVE: Watershops Pond with Arcadia Blvd. to Agnes St. with Island Pond Rd. to the right of the photo shows path of the tornado by the blue tarp roofs. *Photo by John Suchocki*

LEFT: Union Street and George Street, West Springfield. *Photo by John Suchocki*

FAR LEFT: Severe building damage and ongoing demolition of the Main Street in Springfield South End. *Photo by John Suchocki*

ABOVE: Tornado damage in Sturbridge along Main Street (Route 131). *Photo by John Suchocki*

RIGHT: Aerial view of the Veterans Golf Course damage from the tornado the day before. *Photo by John Suchocki*

OPPOSITE: Tornado damage to private aircraft at the Southbridge Municipal Airport. *Photo by John Suchocki*

BELOW: Quinebaug Cove Campground destroyed by the tornado.

Photo by John Suchocki

ABOVE: Monson home damaged. *Photo by John Suchocki*

RIGHT: West Springfield Union Street. *Photo by John Suchocki*

FAR RIGHT: Brimfield Village Campground five days later where a women, Ginger Darlow, was killed by the tornado. *Photo by John Suchocki*

ABOVE: Devastation along Hollow Road in Brimfield. *Photo by John Suchocki*

ABOVE: Tornado damage in the Monson area. *Photo by John Suchocki*

ABOVE LEFT: Tornado damage in the Monson area near East Hill Road. *Photo by John Suchocki*

LEFT: Homes on Bethany Road in Monson, destroyed by the June 1st tornado. *Photo by John Suchocki*

ABOVE: Tornado damage to the Springfield Boys Club Camp in Brimfield off Rout 20. *Photo by John Suchocki*

OPPOSITE: Tornado damage to camping trailers in the Brimfield campgrounds in Brimfield where a women was killed. *Photo by John Suchocki*

ABOVE: Claude and Roberta Cyr spend time with their pets after being displaced by the tornado from their Winton Street, Springfield, home. The animals are being cared for at the T J O'Connor animal shelter. Animals from left to right are, Buffy and Peewee. *Photo by Don Treeger*

ABOVE: A car crushed by a house on Hill Street Wednesday, damaged by the June 1 tornado in the Merrick section of West Springfield. *Photo by Michael S. Gordon*

LEFT: Work continues on the International House residence hall at Springfield College damaged by the June 1 tornado that ripped through the area. *Photo by Michael S. Gordon*

ABOVE: Massachusetts State Treasurer Steve Grossman, left chairman of the Massachusetts School Building Authority, and Springfield Superintendent of School Alan Ingram walk down a second floor hallway of the Brookings School at 367 Hancock, they are passing by a wall that had blown out into the hallway, as was some of the damage caused by last week's tornado. *Photo by Mark Murray*

RIGHT: Madeline R. Zorzi, owner of South Commons Condominium Association at 959-991 Main Street in the South End, talks about her properties now being demolished after they were damaged beyond repair during the June 1 tornado. *Photo by Michael S. Gordon*

BELOW: Eileen and John Moore stand behind their home on Roosevelt Avenue in Springfield which was hit by the tornado on June 1st. Eileen was able to save one of her birdhouse as the rest of her collection was destroyed. *Photo by Mark Murray*

ABOVE: Kenneth A. Newell, day custodian at the Munger Hill Elementary School shows the clock that used to hang in this kindergarten classroom and was blown off the wall during the June 1 tornado. It stopped when the batteries were knocked out of it and they are keeping it as a reminder of the storm. *Photo by Michael S. Gordon*

ABOVE: Katherine Craven, Executive Director of the Massachusetts Building Authority, checks the roof which blew off the Mary Dryden School at 190 Surrey Road, and landed across the street on the side of Cathedral High School on Wendover Road, following last weeks tornado. The agency had paid for this roof which was just installed last year. She was on a tour of Dryden and Brookings School Wednesday with State Treasurer Steve Grossman. *Photo by Mark Murray*

LEFT: Graduate Vincent Zanetti gives a thumbs up while following class marshall Danielle Vear at the 2011 graduation of Monson High School at Wednesday evening's ceremonies at the Granite Valley Middle School. *Photo by Dave Roback*

OPPOSITE: At the lemonade stand on Springfield Street in Chicopee from left family friend Edward Lozado, Heather Paul holding Nathan Paul, age 4, Emily Paul, age 8 and Anna Paul, age 10 man the booth in Chicopee on Wednesday. Proceeds go to the tornado victims.

Photo by Dave Roback

ABOVE: Governor Deval Patrick speaks to West Springfield people effected by the tornado, during a meeting at Coburn School. *Photo by Mark Murray*

ABOVE: A sign of thanks in front of the Brimfield house at 71 Haynes Hill Road damaged by the June 1 tornado. *Photo by Michael S. Gordon*

ABOVE: Mobile homes and recreational vehicles at the Quinebaug Cove Campground damaged by the June 1 tornado.

Photo by Michael S. Gordon

RIGHT: A neighborhood on Main Street damaged by the June 1 tornado. *Photo by Michael S. Gordon*

LEFT: The wreckage of the recreational vehicle belonging to Richard R. Reim, 52, he shared with Virginia L. 'Ginger' Darlow, 52. Reim was injured and Darlow died in the RV during the June 1 tornado in Brimfield. Reim is recuperating at the East Longmeadow Skilled Nursing Home from his injuries. *Photo sumitted by Richard R. Reim*

BELOW: In the foreground is the Jeep belonging to Richard R. Reim. *Photo by Richard R. Reim*

ABOVE: Governor Deval Patrick, right checks out the mortarboard made out of paper being worn by Christopher Lisojo 11, a 5th grader at the Brookings School, as Christopher had just come from the 5th grade graduation ceremony at his school that was hit by the June 1st tornado. His family was also displaced by the tornado when their home was damaged. The Governor was in Court Square for a press conference about the recent federal disaster aid announcement. *Photo by Mark Murray*

RIGHT: Leon Jenkins, left and his brother Walter Jenkins, right, on hand for the arrival Wednesday morning of two temporary house trailers being installed next to their building at 18-20 Searle Place which was damaged in the June 1st tornado. The homes came from American Mobile Homes of Weymouth Mass. *Photo by Mark Murray*

ABOVE: A home on Pleasant Street, Southbridge damaged by the June 1 tornado. *Photo by Michael S. Gordon*

ABOVE LEFT: The Days Inn on Haynes Road in Sturbridge damaged by the June 1 tornado. *Photo by Michael S. Gordon*

LEFT: The Days Inn was sliced in two by the June 1 tornado.

Photo by Michael S. Gordon

ABOVE: Wrecked small airplanes at the Southbridge Municipal Airport damaged by the June 1 tornado. *Photo by Michael S. Gordon*

ABOVE: A Sturbridge neighborhood on Main Street damaged by the June 1 tornado. *Photo by Michael S. Gordon*

OPPOSITE TOP: Trees and houses in the Southbridge neighborhoods around Worcester Street damaged by the June 1 tornado. *Photo by Michael S. Gordon*

OPPOSITE BOTTOM: A view of Brimfield's Paige Hill Road with houses and trees damaged during the June 1 tornado. Hundreds of broken trees are now being cleared from the once heavily wooded area. *Photo by Michael S. Gordon*

ABOVE: Home destroyed on King Street in Monson. *Photo by John Suchocki*

ABOVE: Michael Roescher is on what were the front steps of the home he lived in on Washington Street in Monson. The board shows photos of his seven cats that have been recovered following the tornado of June 1st, and the dates they were found. *Photo by Don Treeger*

RIGHT: Monson resident Pat Nothe of Monson, left and Corey Somerville of the Behavior Health Networks tramatic Response Team works stocking up an outpost at Upper Hampden Road in Monson.

Photo by Dave Roback

FAR RIGHT: A collection bucket sits out in front of 244 East Old Streetrbridge Road in Brimfield looking for donations to help in the tornado relief effort.

Photo by Dave Roback

BELOW: Jeannette Smith, Jessalee Drake, Sue Lucia, and Judy Deane, right, all from the Heritage Baptist Church work to hand out food, water and other items to tornado victims in the area of Island Pond Road, Springfield. The items were dropped off at their church at 640 Plumtree Road, and they are then distributed by the church volunteers. *Photo by Mark Murray*

DONATE!! TORNADO RELIEF FOR 244 EAST OLD STURBRIDGE RD

ABOVE: Trees down on River Street in Agawam shortly after the tornado passed on Wednesday.

Photo by Dave Roback

RIGHT: Lisa Jones, a school adjustment counselor at the Mary Dryden School, holds hands with Zaida Streeteit, a first grader at the Dryden School, who is holding a giant teddy bear which her family rescued when they found him near the Dryden School, following the tornado last week, They have named him Tornado T. The family hopes to reunite the bear with its original owner. They are walking into the Frederick Harris School which they have been relocated to following tornado damage to the Dryden School. *Photo by Mark Murray*

ABOVE: Ken Cregg, a lineman for Verizon out of Dracut, Ma., installs wiring on a new utility pole in the area between Hickory and Melrose Street damaged by the June 1 tornado that ripped through the Springfield. *Photo by Michael S. Gordon*

LEFT: Hampden District Attorney Mark G. Mastoianni checks on the condition of the ceiling in the Massachusetts State Police office in the district attorney's office complex annex at 55 State Street. The building was damaged during the June 1 tornado and the staff is moving to a nearby office building while repairs are made. *Photo by Michael S. Gordon*

ABOVE: Gianna M. Allentuck, the adjustment counselor at the Elias Brookings School in Springfield adding to a garage full of clothes and personal items for the children and families of the school affected by the recent tornado. *Photo by Michael S. Gordon*

LEFT: Relief Coordinator City Solicitor Lisa A. Ball takes a donation for the Paper Cities tornado relief collection for Springfield from Holyoke resident Tammy Leichsenring at Holyoke City hall. *Photo by John Suchocki*

ABOVE: Congressman Richard E. Neal, speaks at the podium, as Springfield Mayor Domenic J. Sarno, left and Governor Deval Patrick, right listen, along with other State and City officials during a press conference in Court Square, Thursday about the recent federal disaster aid announcement for communities hit by the June 1st tornado.

Photo by Mark Murray

RIGHT: Tornado victims Sabina Acharya holding her niece Jenny Sanyasi, 1, as she listens to Governor Deval Patrick speak to people effected by the tornado, during a meeting at Coburn School Friday morning. *Photo by Mark Murray*

FAR RIGHT: Motorist make their way down Main Street near Union Street as one lane of traffic in each direction was re-opened Tuesday afternoon as crews continue to clean up following the June 1st tornado. *Photo by Mark Murray*

ABOVE: A collaborative of tree service companies are bringing trees and brush blown down by the June 1 tornado to a field on Boston Road near Post Office Square in Wilbraham to be mulched. *Photo by Michael S. Gordon*

RIGHT: A mountain of wood chips dwarfs workers at the Wilbraham site. *Photo by Michael S. Gordon*

ABOVE: Crews from Associated Wrecking finished taking down this brick apartment building on Central Street after it received heavy damage from the tornado last week.

Photo by Mark Murray

ABOVE: Comedian Bill Cosby talks with Lisa Michaud, spokesperson for the American Red Cross and Rick Lee, American Red Cross Pioneer Valley Chapter Executive Director, during his visit to Springfield to speak to those sheltered at the MassMutual Center. *Photo by Lucila Santana*

LEFT: Recovery efforts are underway in Brimfield following the tornado of June 1st, 2011. The Village Green Family Campground was decimated by the tornado, but residents and owners are trying to recover. This is a view of where Virginia Darlow, 52, was killed at the campground and her boyfriend, Richard Reim, 51, suffered back and neck injuries when their camper (center rear) flipped upside down. *Photo by Don Treeger*

BELOW LEFT: West Springfield Deputy Chief Streetve Manchino serves up pancakes at the fund-raiser for tornado victims pancake breakfast hosted by the West Springfield firefighters at the Firehouse Restaurant. *Photo by David Molnar*

BELOW RIGHT: Recovery efforts are underway in Brimfield following the tornado of June 1st, 2011. The Village Green Family Campground was decimated by the tornado, but residents and owners are trying to recover. This van was damaged during the tornado. *Photo by Don Treeger*

RIGHT: From left, Melanie Sartori, of Monson, sells 'Monson Unites' T-shirts with her children, David, 9, Symantha, 11, at the Quaoboag Riders tornado relief event Saturday in Monson. *Photo by Lori Stabile*

FAR RIGHT: Richard Kozinski, left chairman of the West Springfield Historical Commission, and Bill Whitney, right, also a member of the commission, look over some of the damage from the June 1st tornado at the cemetery at Union and Church Street. It is one of the oldest cemeteries in the town. *Photo by Mark Murray*

BELOW RIGHT: Children from the Church of Jesus Christ of Latter-Day Saints are shown here participating in a church-sponsored work group to aid victims of the June 1 tornado in the Plumtree Road area of Springfield. *Photo by Don Treeger*

ABOVE: Work continues on the Adams Hometown Market at 115 Main Street in Monson, the store has been closed since the June 1st tornado. *Photo by Mark Murray*

LEFT: Mike Czarnecki checks the stock at the Adams Hometown Market at 115 Main Street in Monson. *Photo by Mark Murray*

RIGHT TOP: Jose Ferreira, stands next to his destroyed home at 14 Mary Street off Island Pond Road in Springfield. The home is going to have to be torn down and rebuilt. *Photo by Mark Murray*

RIGHT BOTTOM: Recovery efforts are underway in Brimfield following the tornado of June 1st, 2011. The Village Green Family Campground was decimated by the tornado, but residents and owners are trying to recover. Here, Robert J. Parron of Holland works on building a new pavilion to replace the one that was destroyed. *Photo by Don Treeger*

BELOW: Workers from the Charlie Arment Trucking work on removing some of the remaining walls to the building at 947 Main Street which housed Square One day care center, it was destroyed in the June 1st tornado. *Photo by Mark Murray*

ABOVE: Derrick Klezos, left, and Steve Young of Patrick Kelly Roofing and Siding of Westfield work to repair a home on Harvest Moon Lane in the Munger Hill section of Westfield damaged during the June 1 tornado. *Photo by Michael S. Gordon*

RIGHT: Nelida Macias, holds a letter she received at her home at 362 Stapleton Road, Springfield which received tornado damage, the note was from the previous owner and also attached $200 to help pay for some of the damages. *Photo by Mark Murray*

BELOW LEFT: Sonia Burke from the Pioneer Valley Red Cross hugs Deborah Flores as she was one of the last tornado victims to leave the MassMutual Shelter which closed Wednesday. *Photo by Mark Murray*

BELOW MIDDLE: FEMA workers Magda Reyes, left and Tomas Rivera, right, talk with home owner Celeste Femia, in front of her tornado damaged home on Arcadia Blvd., as they were out talking with homeowners and letting them know they should sign up with FEMA to help cover some of their expenses. *Photo by Mark Murray*

BELOW RIGHT: A house on Charlton Street, Southbridge, damaged by the June 1 tornado. *Photo by Michael S. Gordon*

ABOVE: Grazia Caputo, left holds a sign as Kathy Caputo, right, lets everyone know that the Red Rose Pizzeria is open again after being closed for a week following the tornado.

Photo by Mark Murray

LEFT: Crane on State Street used to remove and replace tornado damaged air conditioning units on the roof of 95 State Street. *Photo by John Suchocki*

143

A Team Effort!

Thank You! ... to a great group of dedicated employees, an understanding public, and to our local fire, police, and inspectional services employees.

A message from Columbia Gas of Massachusetts President, Stephen H. Bryant

The devastation of the June 1st tornadoes and the damage to the natural gas system was unprecedented. Our employees from Western Massachusetts, along with crews from our Brockton and Lawrence service areas, worked around the clock for days on end to secure the system and ensure the safety of the public. I have never been prouder of them.

We also need to express our gratitude to the public – customers and non-customers – in the stricken areas, for your patience and understanding. You were a great help and encouragement to our employees.

And lastly, we all need to thank the fire, police, and inspectional services department employees from throughout Western Mass. They were asked to manage a tragic situation, and they did it brilliantly.

The response to the storm of June 1st was a collective effort of teamwork, compassion and selflessness, which all of Western Massachusetts can take great pride in.

Columbia Gas®
of Massachusetts

A NiSource Company